Analyze Your Own Script Workshop – THE BOOK

The Master Toolbox For Strengthening Weak Areas and Discovering Hidden Treasures Buried Inside Your Screenplay

by Melody Jackson

Analyze Your Own Script Workshop – THE BOOK

The Master Toolbox For Strengthening Weak Areas and Discovering Hidden Treasures Buried Inside Your Screenplay

Publisher

Live Your Great Life Enterprises
4335 Van Nuys Blvd. #322
Sherman Oaks, CA 91403
(818) 907-6511
support@smartg.com
http://smartg.com
https://hollywoodbschool.com

Follow us on Twitter: **https://twitter.com/smartgirlspr**
Like **Smart Girls Productions** on Facebook: **https://www.facebook.com/SmartGirlsProductions/**
Like **Hollywood Business School** on Facebook: **https://www.facebook.com/hollywoodbschool/**

A Free Gift For You

Thank you for purchasing this workshop-in-a-book!

Please get your FREE subscription to our weekly publication of **Marketing Caffeine for Screenwriters**,

In the Marketing Caffeine weekly content series, you will learn how the business of screenwriting really works in Hollywood while also getting bite-sized tips to improve your screenwriting skills.

Each weekly shot of our Marketing Caffeine on Screenwriting is designed to educate, motivate, and call you into action.

Go to our website now to get it now to get it at:

http://smartg.com/screenwriters/marketing-caffeine

Each week you'll get a bite-sized email about that week's article, video, or podcast. Then just click to get your double-strength shot of Marketing Caffeine to keep yourself inspired, motivated, and up-to-date all the time.

Dedication And Thank You

This book is dedicated to all of the screenwriting clients I've worked with over the last 20-plus years in helping them with their screenplays.

Writing a screenplay requires an enormous amount of time, not to mention opening up your heart and soul just to get your story on the page.

It's been a pleasure, an honor, and a lot of fun to help these screenwriters get their story that lies deep within them onto the page. I admire their commitment and dedication to doing whatever it takes to complete a screenplay. Even further, I salute each of them for the courage it took to put themselves on the line when they sent me their screenplay for feedback. As writers and artists, it's not always easy to ask for feedback and for someone to tell you what's wrong with the project you just put an enormous amount of energy and time into. But that's what real writers do.

I see all of my clients as courageous creative warriors.

I also want to thank the forefathers and foremothers in script analysis from whose books and courses I learned so much, each of whom presented ways of breaking down a script and building it back up in their own unique ways. Some of those influences who particularly stand out for me are Linda Seger, John Truby, Syd Field, and Robert McKee. I have great respect for them all.

From understanding their theories and methods, bringing my own discoveries from analyzing over 2500 scripts, and mixing in relevant insights from my studies of Joseph Campbell and Carl Jung, I hope that the tools in this book may be a unique complement to the great screenwriting books and tools already created.

Dr. Melody Jackson is the founder of the Hollywood Business School and the Hollywood marketing firm Smart Girls Productions.

Melody has helped thousands of clients move forward to the next level in their Hollywood careers.

For more information on marketing and consulting services for screenwriters offered by Smart Girls Productions, go to **smartg.com**.

To learn what courses are available for screenwriters, visit the site of the Hollywood Business School at **HollywoodBschool.com**.

My Philosophy and Approach

Hello!

I'm Melody Jackson, the author of this book and the founder of two businesses -- the marketing and branding firm **Smart Girls Productions** and the educational website **Hollywood Business School**. In the next page or two, I'm going to tell you about my background so you know how I got to the point of creating the tools in this book to help you do a self-analysis on your script before sending it to a professional. To accomplish this, I'm going to jam-pack relevant highlights of my experience into the following two pages.

Originally from the Midwest, I earned a bachelor's degree in Computer Science – this was great fuel for the analytical and systems part of my brain which wrote this book! While earning my B.S. I also studied business, contemporary dance, and the humanities and loved them all! The point is that, even from my early education, I felt naturally compelled to nurture both my analytical side and my creative, right brain. I loved computers and technology and was also very engaged and interested in the humanities and the study of how human beings express themselves creatively.

After college I moved to California and worked for the U.S. Department of Defense at a missile/rocket defense operation. After only a year, I knew I wanted to do something more exciting. Like.... SELLING computers!

I immediately went to work as a salesperson at a computer store and loved it. It was a perfect marriage of my technical skills and my passion for marketing – which, as it turns out, is my creative expression.

As I continued to sell computers and equipment at other companies, somewhere along the way, I began studying acting and screenwriting. After studying intensively, working hard and marketing myself in both areas for seven years, I was clear I didn't want to be an actor or screenwriter myself, but I enjoyed the business of it. And that time, Smart Girls Productions was already thriving.

Essentially, I had arrived at the same place I had started – doing work that merged my left and right brain skills and interests together.

The inquiry for me has always been: ***"What systems and methods can be created to assure you develop a strong foundation that will free you up to do your most authentic and creative work?"***

I believe if you methodically identify what is needed to create a strong foundation in any type of artistic work, then – and only then – can the most artistic, creative, non-linear expression of the artist/writer emerge. The tools in this book are exactly that. They will help you create a strong foundation on which to hang your greatest creativity and unique vision.

While running Smart Girls Productions for the past 20+ years, I've helped more than 10,000 actors and screenwriters. Along the way, I earned my Ph.D. in Mythological Studies, ran two marathons, and traveled a good deal. Although some people tell me I work too much, I actually do have a life outside of work. I tell you this because I think having a full life is important for everyone – especially if you do creative work because it gives you juice to draw from!

A couple more things about my background:
- In three separate surveys over an 11-year period, I was named one of the **Top 5 Script Consultants** in the U.S. by a top industry magazine.
- For a period of four years, I led seminars for one of the leading personal development companies in the world.

All of these things have impacted my thinking and perspective. Most importantly, I think the blend of my particular set of skills, passions, and experience has put me in a unique position for writing this workshop-in-a-book. My analytical side helped me create tools to methodically guide you to create a strong foundation for your story. My creative side and background in mythology, psychology and the humanities have contributed the sensibility needed to ask questions that can help you get to the emotion, feelings and more elusive aspects of a story that moves people.

I hope you find this to be true as you delve into using it to take your screenplay to its greatest potential. Enjoy this book and may it call you to action and inspire you about your screenplay!

My email address is support@smartg.com if you need anything.

Cheers,

Melody Jackson

CONTENTS

WHO THIS WORKBOOK IS FOR

This workbook is for screenwriters who already have some understanding of how to write a screenplay and are looking to develop a new idea for a script, to rewrite an existing screenplay, or to polish a screenplay they've already rewritten extensively.

This workbook is also ideal for screenplay professionals and filmmakers who want to make their scripts sound more fresh or to polish their scripts at a whole new level of creativity.

This workbook is **not** for learning how to format a screenplay. It's **not** for learning how to get started in a screenwriting career, and it **does not teach how to begin writing a screenplay**.

It is designed to be a support structure and script analysis toolbox for screenwriters. For aspiring screenwriters still working on their first script, it can also be used as a complement to other courses and books that teach the foundations of screenwriting.

THE PURPOSE OF THIS WORKBOOK

Writing a solid screenplay has so many moving elements that it's impossible for most people to keep track of everything in their heads. This workbook takes the complex project of a script that is created from the right brain and helps you break it down methodically from many different angles so you can more easily see what aspects need development. It will also help you analyze how the key elements of your script integrate with each other.

The tools you'll find here are intended to stimulate your thoughts by asking you probing questions to help you flesh out where things are missing. You'll also see some graphs and charts to make some aspects of the development more visual.

Overall, this workbook will help you plan, organize, and evaluate your thoughts and ideas for your screenplay. You can use it at any point in the development of your script, whether you're in the earliest stages and still thinking your story through or you're at the point where you want to do one last pass to polish it.

THE THREE MAJOR PHASES
OF SCRIPT DEVELOPMENT

The three main phases of script development are Idea Development, Rewriting, and Polishing. The tools in this workbook will help you no matter which phase of development you're in. You may just need to change the tense of the verbs in some cases since some questions are worded as if you are just beginning to write the story and, in other cases, the questions are worded as if you're analyzing what you've already written. The tools will work the same way in all cases -- just change the verb tense in your mind! Here's a little more on how the tools help you in the various phases.

Phase 1 - Idea Development through Completing the First Draft

When you plan your story out and think through many of the key elements ahead of time, it can save lots of headaches later. You can use this workbook to guide you through one of the greatest challenges of screenwriting – getting the critical elements of your screenplay to overlap, connect, integrate, and work together.

A second way the workbook is valuable in this phase is to have one hard copy workbook for each of the main stories you're working on. Many screenwriters have too many ideas to write a screenplay for each idea. By using the tools in this workbook for each of your main ideas, you can start to flesh them out and think them through more fully. In turn, that could help you decide which one has the most potential and which one you really, in your heart, want to write.

Phase 2 - Rewriting

Once you have completed a decent first draft, which, in some ways, is the hardest part of screenwriting since you're creating it from scratch, then you face a big challenge of a different type. This next big challenge is getting all of the key elements (character arcs, plot structure, theme, dialogue, and relationships) working in unison as one great story.

The nearly 50 tools in this workbook are designed to help you connect the lines between these many elements as you decide you want to use them. You don't have to use all of the tools, you can just pick and choose certain ones as you need to work on that element. It's like having a coach in your pocket.

If you know your character arc is not where it needs to be, you can go to that tool to work it through instead of just randomly rewriting it in your script.
This will not only save you a great deal of time compared to just trying to manage what needs to

be done in your head, but it will also help you be much more methodical about implementing it.

Phase 3 – Polishing

After you've completed a solid second draft or more and your script is in pretty good shape but you want to take it off the charts, this is where the tools really start to fly!

You can use this workbook as a checklist for your screenplay and and choose which tools you want to pull out of the toolbox to take your script over the top.

One example of this is the dialogue tool. Dialogue is often troublesome and typically needs a fair amount of work even in a script that's a few drafts down the road.

You could go to one of the *Dialogue Profiles* in here and fill it out for any character you want to focus on to really punch up their dialogue. Do it for each of your main characters and you'll have authentic, distinct, revealing dialogue that will make each of them memorable.

With around 50 tools, you will find the perfect questions to help you analyze your own script to see where the weakness are and how to polish it to fulfill its potential.

~~~

This workbook will help you develop your script as far as you can on your own, which can potentially save you thousands of dollars that you might otherwise spend having professional script analysts give you feedback.

Once you get your script as far as you can, however, I still recommend you to go to a professional analyst so you can get an outside opinion on how it all comes together. This is important because as writers, we sometimes have worked on something so much that we can no longer see what is missing. Our minds play tricks on us and we fill in blanks or still see things we might have cut out along the way!

No matter what, you will be much further along in your developing your script and taking it to its fullest potential.

~~~

A couple of final notes on using the tools in this workbook.

This workbook is oriented around a single protagonist *(one main character)*, but for stories like buddy pictures and ensembles which have multiple protagonists, you can write your answers to the questions on separate documents for the relevant forms.

The approach to structure in these tools centers around the three-act structure, but the tools are also easily adapted to use for analyzing any kind of structure breakdown. In fact, you'll see that in many cases, the structure is broken down into quarters – which also happens to align with the three-act structure. The first 25% is the first act; the second 25% is the first half of the second act; the third 25% is the second half of the second act; and the fourth 25% is the third act. Bottom-line, every plot structure will happen somewhere on the timeline, so you readily use the tools for any type of breakdown.

~~~

To make the tools flow as easily as possible, I've chosen to use his and her and their interchangeably to refer to a given character. That is all on that.

~~~

If you are new to screenwriting, you will be reassured by the questions herein that it is a complex process. As with any craft, you get better by doing the thing itself and focusing on improving your skills.

Because of the wide variance in the way professionals use related terms, a short glossary is included at the end to clarify the definitions I'm using in this workbook.

To reiterate, this workbook is not intended to replace screenwriting classes, books, or professional script consultants, but it will serve as a great guide for helping you fulfill your script's potential.

Good luck as you ponder your ideas, fill in the blanks, refine your skills, and develop your script. Let's get to the tools!

Melody Jackson, Ph.D.

General Thoughts and Ideas

CHECKLIST

Use this checklist to see how far along you are in completing your workbook. It's not necessary to complete all of the forms inside but if you do, it's more likely that you'll have a fully-fleshed out story with interesting characters and a transformative experience for your audience.

- ☐ Story Presentation
- ☐ Why Are You Writing This Story?
- ☐ Main Character - Objective Profile
- ☐ Position in Life Statement
- ☐ Main Character – Subjective Profile
- ☐ 3-D Main Character Map
- ☐ Relating to the Main Character
- ☐ Empathy Tracking
- ☐ Protagonist Dialogue Characterization
- ☐ Protagonist Sample Dialogue
- ☐ Character Dimensions Map – Other Characters
- ☐ Opponent / Antagonist – Total Profile
- ☐ Opponent / Antagonist – Dialogue Profile
- ☐ Love Interest /Ally– Total Profile
- ☐ Love Interest /Ally – Dialogue Profile
- ☐ Ally / Friend – Total Profile
- ☐ Ally / Friend – Dialogue Profile
- ☐ Relationship Map
- ☐ Feelings Progression Snapshot – Main Character to Supporting Character #1
- ☐ Feelings Progression Snapshot – Main Character to Supporting Character #2
- ☐ Feelings Progression Snapshot – Supporting Character #1 to Main Character
- ☐ Feelings Progression Snapshot – Supporting Character #2 to Main Character
- ☐ General Dialogue Analysis Tool
- ☐ Character Authentication Tool
- ☐ Plot Point Brainstorm
- ☐ Structure – Plot & Subplot Storylines – Things That Happen
- ☐ Sequences

- [ ] Story Structure Narrative Breakdown
- [ ] Subplot Analysis
- [ ] Subplot Support to Main Plot Analysis
- [ ] Graph of Structure – Moments of Change
- [ ] Story Setup and Payoff Checkup
- [ ] Beyond Cliche – Bringing a Scene to Life
- [ ] Emotional Flame-Thrower
- [ ] Conflict Escalator
- [ ] Doubling The Jeopardy
- [ ] Raising the Stakes Planner
- [ ] Writing Stylizer
- [ ] Creativity Toolbox
- [ ] Symbolism – Metaphors – Visuals
- [ ] Making Locations Work For Your Story
- [ ] Five Key Locations
- [ ] Location Sensation Tool
- [ ] Making Your Story Thematic and Cinematic
- [ ] Making Your Story Visual and Thematic
- [ ] Production Values
- [ ] Commercial Positioning
- [ ] Market Appeal
- [ ] Script Format & Styling Analysis

THE WORKBOOK IS FOR
MY SCREENPLAY TITLED

_____

Write Your Working Title

General Thoughts and Ideas

Story Overview, Meaning, and Theme

STORY PRESENTATION

FUNCTION OF THE TOOL

This tool helps you think through the broad strokes, the basic overview of your story.

This purpose of this tool is also to keep you on track with the big picture of your story. You can think through your premise, storyline, themes, and hook to give you direction at the start, then allow it to evolve as the story flows along and begins to speak to you.

You can also record your working title and any other title ideas you have. As your story unfolds through the process of working on it, you will likely get fresh ideas on what it's really about.

A phrase here or a concept there may occur to you as the perfect title as you continue to work on your script. Record those ideas here so you have lots of ideas by the time you have to choose your title and send your script out.

Story Presentation

THE TOOL

What is your Working Title? What are other possible titles? Feel free to list possible words that might be worth considering using in the title. Brainstorm and use this as a workspace for your title.

What issues and topics are brought up in your story? What **Themes** recur in the story?

What is the simple basic **Concept** of your story, stated as simply as possible, with a small number of words, while still conveying the main action of the story? Not the plot, but the main storyline action?

What is the **Premise** of your story? What truth comes through? What message does your story reveal about the themes and issues it touches on?

What is the **Hook** in your story? What is the catchy, unique circumstance that will interest people in seeing the movie?

Notes and Ideas

What would the super short TV GUIDE listing say? The basic idea?

What is your LOGLINE? (One or two sentences. Write two or three possibilities.

Write your STORY in one paragraph. Include a beginning, middle, and end and incorporate the main characters, conflict, setting, and theme.

WHY ARE YOU WRITING THIS STORY?

FUNCTION OF THE TOOL

Setting out on the journey to write a screenplay is a huge commitment that will take hundreds of hours, and if it's gonna be a good script, it will require you put your heart and soul in it, that you tap into a universal truth that is within you – **something you know to be true about life** -- that others can identify with.

The power of art -- in any form -- is that it metaphorically reflects a truth about the human experience that words alone can't fully describe. Even the **words** in a novel are not just words -- they tell a story to express the truth -- the story is the art.

The artist or writer presents their truth to other human beings through their work and says, *"This is how it is. This art piece right here... This is reflecting some truth about the human experience that I know to be true."*

Even when you write a light fare story about teenagers at a haunted house or a road comedy, if it is to be worthwhile, at least a grain of truth about the human experience must come through. Not truth as in being real in life, but in **the sense of the feelings and situations that we experience as human beings.**

By exploring more deeply why your story means something to you – whether you do it just as you start writing your script, somewhere in the middle of your process, or when you've finished yet another draft – you will definitely find that you have been moved to share a truth about the experience of being human. Otherwise you wouldn't have been inspired to write it. That truth might be deeply spiritual and transcendent, it might be sad laughter about the frailties of old age, or it could simply be a funny reflection that offers audiences relief from the tension in their everyday lives as they laugh and say, "Yes! I know what you mean."

This tool will help you clearly identify **why** you wanted to write this screenplay. It will help you put into words the observation, truth, or message you want to share and why you think it's so valuable, interesting or helpful that you are willing to dedicate untold hours of your life to writing it.

Ultimately, this is meant to help you keep clear on why you want to say and to capture your idea of why you decided to write it.

Why Are You Writing This Story?

THE TOOL

Why is it important to you to write this story? How strongly do you feel about it? Do you care deep down about the material?

What are you trying to say as a writer or artist? (Reference your themes.) Do you really believe this message?

What is your new insight into the problem or issue presented in your story?

What do you want the audience to feel when the story ends? What is the main thing you need to do to make sure they feel this at the end?

Why did you choose to write about this character? Why do you think this is a realistic character? Why is this character the best one to show what you want to say?

What do you ultimately want out of writing this screenplay? What is your main reason for writing it? What do you intend to do with it when you finish?

Development of Characters

APPROACH TO YOUR CHARACTERS

Before we jump into the character tools, I want to lay some groundwork for how we are approaching character breakdowns, starting with the use of certain terms.

The **Main Character** or **Hero** in classical drama is known as the **Protagonist.** In my original version of this workbook, I used only the term **Protagonist** since it's the proper literary term. But after giving it what has probably been too much thought, in this new updated version of the book, I've decided to use the three terms interchangeably, namely because they have slightly different connotations and sometimes one feels more right or sounds better than the others. The fact that I labored over that choice brings up a point about my approach to this entire book... or really, I should say, your analysis of your screenplay.

Your job is to make people feel something -- to get your audience out of their heads and into a *feeling space*.

All the structuring and development work you do on your script is in service of making your audience **FEEL** something. It's not easy to do – and that's exactly why I created every tool in this book – to help you write in a way that makes the reader FEEL your story.

Going back to which words to use to refer to the protagonist. On one hand I'm a purist who likes to use the correct terms of art because they often have subtle implications. Yet sometimes, a different term just feels right. You may have a preference or not. For our purposes, substitute whatever term is most helpful in stimulating your imagination. Likewise, I will use the terms Antagonist and Opponent interchangeably.

Another type of role in film is a Supporting Role. The supporting role is a secondary character such as the love interest or the key character in a subplot. The forms on the following pages are for working on these various types of characters. Here's a short reference for the synonyms I may use:

- Protagonist = Main Character, Leading Character, Hero
- Antagonist = Opponent, Adversary
- Supporting Character = Secondary Role, Love Interest, Buddy, Ally

One more important topic to cover before we jump in.

The Three Dimensions of Characters

Lajos Egri writes in his book *The Art of Dramatic Writing* that a character has three dimensions--physical, sociological, and psychological--the psychological being the product of the other two. Syd Field, the author of the seminal work *Screenplay*, identifies the three dimensions of a character as the professional, personal, and private.

Yet another theory breaks characters down into the three dimensions of Intellectual, Physical, and Emotional.

The point is you can break down the qualities of character in a variety of ways. You could come up with hundreds of possible qualities – or continuums of qualities – that you could use to describe your character creations.

But for a screenplay, you don't need to know every single thing about the character. You simply need to have a strong sense of exactly who your character is in the areas that are relevant to this story. For instance, you don't need to know what his third grade teacher was like unless it impacts your story.

It's good, however, for your character to have dimension... to not just be flat. With the character tools offered here, you can pick and choose qualities to add dimension however you like. Make up whatever you want... as long as the qualities create a congruent image. Most importantly, when working on a 3-D profile of a character, ***note as many or as few details as is relevant to your story***.

On the next page, you'll see a list of possible qualities you may wish to choose from. On the various Character Profiles, you can then reference this list of qualities to help you brainstorm on who your character is and what qualities may be relevant.

Physical Qualities

The Basics

Gender

Age, Year of Birth

Skin Color

Height and Weight

Hair Color & Style

Eye Color

Glasses, Contacts

Fitness Level, Obese

Appearance

Attractive, Average, Ugly

Unkempt, Tidy, Stylish

Nose, Lips, Cheekbones

Feet, Hands

Tattoos or other Unusual Marks

Deformities

Noticeable Physical Assets

Sociological Qualities

Status – Work - Interests

Money & Social Class

Occupation / Work Situation

Attitude Toward Work

Work Competency

Education - Area of Study, Grades

Aptitudes, I.Q.

Religion, Spiritual Beliefs

Race, Nationality, Political Party

Pastime Activities

Entertainment Preferences

Reading & Musical Tastes

Hobbies & Special Talent

Primary Relationship

Relationship Vibe – Loving, Abusive

Sex Life

Maturity Level

Status of Existing Relationship

Past Marital Status

Significant Past Relationships

Recurring Romantic Problems

Their Parents

Living, Deceased

Separated, Divorced, Remarried, Single

Loving, Abusive

Present, Absent

Expressive, Silent

Socioeconomic Class

Adoptive, Planned, Surprise

Children

Number of Kids or None

Infertile, Regretful, Longing

Relationship to Their Kids

Type of Parent They Are

Psychological Qualities

Sex Life

Moral Standards

Ambition

Life Goal

Fears

Desires

Vices, Bad Habits, Good Habits

Optimistic, Pessimistic

Frustrations, Disappointments

Extrovert, Introvert, Ambivert

Easygoing, Stressed Temperament

Complexes, Issues

Monkey on the Back

Feel free to add to these lists. These lists are a composite of a various lists I've drawn from over years and added my own. Use this list any time you're trying to make a character more interesting or gain insight into what they're all about.

In the following page, you'll specifically address the Main Character stats. Later on, you'll see places to address the qualities of supporting characters, but you won't explore them as much in depth.

MAIN CHARACTER – OBJECTIVE STATS

FUNCTION OF THE TOOL

This tool is to guide you in doing an objective description of the main character. Namely, describe any characteristics of specific importance but only if they matter.

Note physical appearance, social status, past relationships, psychological aspects, and so forth as appropriate.

Avoid stereotypes by breaking them with a non-stereotypic characteristic.

If you're not sure if something you've pictured about your character is important -- or at least relevant -- ask yourself why it *might* be important? What does it reveal about the character? If it doesn't matter from that perspective, either leave that out or just make a choice and come up with another reason it could be relevant. But don't put too many superfluous descriptors. For instance, if you say your character has red hair, does that matter? Even if it just creates a particular vibe of a character, that's fine. It's a good enough reason. But don't make something up just to have it there.

It's up to you to decide.

Fire away.

MAIN CHARACTER - OBJECTIVE PROFILE

THE TOOL

Character Name _____

Physical: What do they look like?

Sociological Stats, Relationships

Psychological

Stereotypes

What aspects of your character might be stereotyped? Which of these stereotypic characteristics hold true in his case? Which ones do not? Which stereotypes do you want to break?

POSITION IN LIFE STATEMENT

Function of the Tool

This is an opportunity to get to know your main character more fully. When you know your character more and explore them more deeply, there's a way in which these new discoveries start to ooze right into the pages of your script or can easily be incorporated to create a much fuller, more interesting character.

For the following questions write about any area of the main character's life which is relevant to the script.

You can focus on the marital status, jobs, children, parents, health, psychological issues or anything you want as it relates to his position in life.

Answer the questions based on what is relevant to your story.

Position In Life Statement

The Tool

What is his/her current position in life?

How did he get there?

How does he feel about where he is in his life?

Where would he like to be or go?

How does he feel about his ability to get there?

Notes and Ideas

MAIN CHARACTER - SUBJECTIVE PROFILE

FUNCTION OF THE TOOL

The function of this tool is to help you get to know your main character better, to get to know them more in depth and to help you make sure there is a character arc, something the main character learns over the course of the story.

To have that happen, the protagonist has to have some kind of problem at the beginning that they need to solve. In fact, there are really two types of problems:

1) an external problem – the main plot revolves around this and the main character is *aware* of this problem;
2) an internal problem – this is a problem the main character has relating to where he/she needs to grow personally to reach the goal in the external plot; they are typically *unaware* of this problem.

For the character arc, the main character must be **<u>unaware</u>** of their real problem at first. They might even think their internal issue is something different than it really is.

As they are **called to action** in the external storyline -- the goal they have in the plot -- that's when they realize their personal issue is getting in the way of them reaching their external goal. That's when the main character has to take on the personal challenge of confronting and resolving their personal issue so they can reach their external goal. Audiences watch to see what they do when they are challenged in this way.

The process of the main character's evolution in this process is the Character Arc.

PROTAGONIST – CHARACTER ARC

THE TOOL

Character Name _____

What is your character's greatest weakness or fault? How does that quality cause him problems in the story? Does it have the potential to destroy him? How close can he get to destruction without falling over the edge? How could you take him that close?

What is your protagonist's immediate goal or desire and why is he driven to fulfill it?

What does your protagonist have at stake that motivates him? How could the stakes be higher?

What is your protagonist's real, underlying need that he doesn't recognize until the end of the story? What lesson does he finally learn by the end of the story as a result of his experiences in the story?

How does the character evolve? What progressive steps does your character take to change from the way he is at the beginning to the end? How is your character different at the end from the beginning?

Where, near the end of the story, is your character's newly learned behavior demonstrated in an old situation? Where are we assured that the change is *going to stick*.

Is your protagonist interesting to watch? Why would people want to know more about her/him? Do you want to keep watching (reading) to find out what happens next?

3-D MAIN CHARACTER

Function of the Tool

The purpose of this tool is to add dimension to your protagonist and make them more interesting. Using this tool has three steps.

- The first step is to identify three separate characteristics of your character so they're not flat. These should be characteristics you want to be noticeable.
- The second step is identify the opportunities/moments in your story where these characteristics can come out.
- The third step is to amplify, exaggerate or make those characteristics more extreme to make the character more interesting and add stakes to the story.

To use it, in the top three lines under where it says "The Tool," write three key qualities of your main character covering different areas of their lives. Then for each of the lines in the circle, write the extreme positive or too much of the quality on one end of the line, and at the other end, write the extreme negative or lack of that quality. (i.e. honest/insensitive, ambitious/ruthless) Then in the box below the circle and lines, write in one of the moments you see that key quality in the story and how you could take it to further out to one extreme or the other. How could these qualities cause him or contribute to conflict? How could they be taken to greater extremes?

An example of a few qualities could be: *likes to have their way, worried, loving, physically fit*. The **_extremes_** of those qualities:
- *likes to have their way*: push-over TO very controlling
- *worried*: doesn't care at all TO a total mess from worrying
- *independent*: completely independent TO totally reliant
- *physically fit*: obsessive gym rat TO a smoker or overweight

The final step is to fill in the box and think of how you could amplify two of those qualities at least a little bit and one of them A LOT! Play around with these to make the character more extreme and interesting!

3-D CHARACTER MAP

The Tool

_____

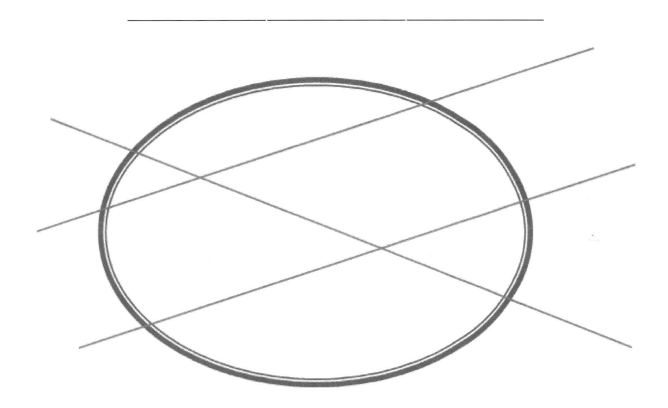

Noticeable Characteristic	Key Moment/s It Shows	How It Could Be Amped Up

RELATING TO THE MAIN CHARACTER

FUNCTION OF THE TOOL

Once you've created a character arc that integrates with the plot – meaning the protagonist evolves as a result of trying to reach the external goal, then we face a second common challenge.

That second big challenge is make the protagonist someone the audience can identify with and relate to.

Your audience needs to be able to identify with *the feelings* of that character. We don't have to have been in the same situation, but we have to identify with the feelings.

Most of us have never been on a battlefield, but we can feel the anguish of loss in the great movie characters we've seen in that situation (*Braveheart, Saving Private Ryan*).

Despite how frequently we see it in movies, most of us haven't reunited with the long-awaited love of our life to walk back off the plane skybridge, but we can *relate* to the idea of finally uniting with a blissful love and getting what we've long for.

This tool will help you make sure your audience can relate to your protagonist by connecting with their feelings.

RELATING TO THE MAIN CHARACTER

THE TOOL

In what ways does the audience identify with this character? What qualities do they see in her or him that they recognize in themselves?

At what moments does the audience feel for, cheer for, or relate to her in some way?

What tiny details reveal something important about your character?

Are you drawing the audience in by revealing more and more interesting things about her as you go along – especially in the first half of your script? Identify the moments where you reveal these things.

At what moments does the audience get an insight into why she is like she is?

Where does the audience fully empathize with your main character's flaws? Are these flaws they can forgive? Do they understand why she is like that?

EMPATHY TRACKING

Function of the Tool

The purpose of this tool is also to make sure audiences feel something for your main character. For audiences to really empathize, they need to see things they like about the character as well as their vulnerabilities.

This tool is related to the one just completed but simply asks the questions in a different way. Answer the following questions any way you choose, from the most superficial qualities to the most profound.

After writing your answers in a narrative form, you'll see a chart where you can actually identify the moments in the script where the these things happen and the audience is able to connect with, feel for, or empathize with your protagonist.

EMPATHY TRACKING

THE TOOL

Main Character Name _____

Why would an audience like your main character? Where do we see good things about him/her? This is the whole essence of what Blake Snyder referred to in "Save the Cat." Your main character does something nice so people like them. List as many reasons as possible. In the table on the next page, you'll get a chance to list the pages you see these on.

What is **not** likable about him? What is his weakness or bad habit? What does he need to learn? Where does he need to grow as a human being? You might reference the 3-D character map for help with this.

Why do we **accept** what's not likable about him? You might help us understand how they got to be that way. Maybe we see them trying not to be that way. Sometimes we accept it because they have so many other good qualities -- even though we wish he/she would change (just like in life)! Why do we accept their character flaw?

When do we empathize with him the most? When do we really feel for them because we see the struggle they are dealing with and we feel badly for him?

Notes and Ideas

This is a continuation of the Empathy Tool. As the column heading says: Reference a key scene or moment, what your protagonist feels, and what emotion that evokes in the audience?

Key Scene/Moment	Protagonist Feels	Audience Emotion

PROTAGONIST - DIALOGUE PROFILE

FUNCTION OF THE TOOL

The number one problem I see with dialogue is that even if the content is there –the information the character needs to convey – the dialogue often has no characterization.

If you think about it, everyone you know in real life has a way they talk, a pattern, a particular vocabulary, words they use a lot! They may have a slight accent. They may be formal in their speech patterns or they may use very few words to convey their ideas.

Everyone has a style of speaking and it's part of what defines them. If your story is about characters from a particular area, they may all have a similar accent with slight variations, even if they have a similar vocabulary. They must however be distinct in how they speak.

Many writers write dialogue for their characters the way they themselves speak. Or sometimes a writer will annoyingly try to force the reader to hear the character's accent and misspell 90% of the words to convey it – that is a very bad idea! (If your character has an accent, simply spell a few words to indicate it – don't overdo it!)

The overall challenge is making the dialogue for each character distinct from the others -- even if most of them are from the same area and have similar accents. This tool will help you define your main character's dialogue. It's a dialogue profile.

It's also important to realize that a character's dialogue style is not defined only by their vocabulary size, accent, and the actual words. Their dialogue indicates their thoughts and is influenced by their view of the person they are talking to, their view of the world, and what's important to them. Think of a doting parent who frequently talks about their child. Or a girl who is always talking about her latest boyfriend who she really thinks this time... he's the one. It's the subject matter that concerns them! In other words, you are creating the personality of the character on multiple levels through their dialogue.

Use the dialogue tool for one character at a time. Here's one for only the main character. There are shorter tools later for some of the supporting characters.

Protagonist - Dialogue Profile

THE TOOL

Character Name _____

What is your main character's dialogue style? Formal? Colloquial? Proper grammar? Uneducated? Adult or child speech pattern? Do you personally know someone like this character? Who can you think of that this character sounds like?

How would you describe your character's speech pattern or rhythm? Dialect? Accent? What distinguishes this character from others?

What distinct or unusual words does this character use? Colloquialisms? Regionalisms? Dialogue tags (overused words or habits)? Is there a general topic or value this character cares about that seems to come up a lot in conversation?

Are there any terms he/she won't use that everyone around him uses? Does he curse? Are there any words of specific importance to them? Any values come through?

Are there any particular subjects this character would never talk about? Is there anything conspicuously unsaid?

Notes and Ideas

Protagonist Sample Dialogue

THE TOOL

Character Name _____

Using the character's dialogue style as you have defined above, write sample dialogue in first person as this character telling how he or she fits in the story. As you get going with it, you'll really flow.

"So there I was...."

Read this dialogue aloud. Does it sound authentic, as a real person would speak? How can you make it more interesting, reveal more character, and cut it down without losing anything?

DIMENSIONS OF OTHER CHARACTERS

Function of the Tool

You've just gone pretty far in depth on your main character. Now we're going to segue to the other characters. To get through the section on your protagonist, you actually had to think through your story quite a bit – and not just on your protagonist.

If you filled in the forms along the way, you actually had to think through other characters to be able to establish certain things about your main character.

Since you probably have a pretty good idea about who your other characters are now, we're going to use these tools in a different order than for the main character. We're going to start with identifying various aspects of your other characters.

The purpose of this tool is to help you develop and make your other characters more interesting. However, for your supporting and featured characters, you only need to identify one or two key qualities about them. You don't need to define and reveal multiple levels of every character, only your main ones.

In the chart below, select **two more** of your major characters and identify three qualities for each of them. Then select two secondary characters to make two-dimensional, and two featured characters and the one main quality you want to make stand out about them. If you have several characters you want to give more definition to, of course, go ahead and do that. Just draw extra lines in which ever circles you want. Use this tool to support the specifics of your story.

This can be a really fun tool to help you get creative and continue to differentiate your characters.

Of course, once you get clear on the qualities, you have to decide where those attributes will come out on the page just like we did with the main character. But you'll have to do that on your own as we're only tracking the **implementation** for the main character.

Character Dimensions

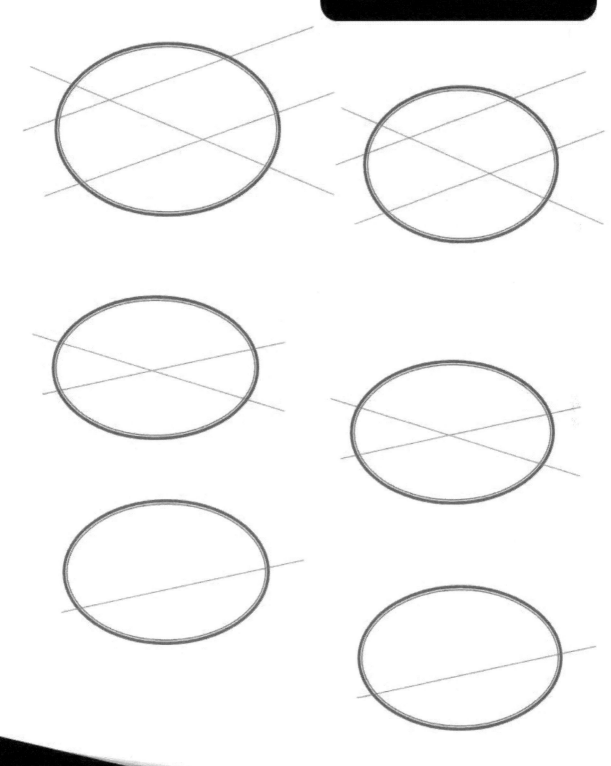

OPPONENT / ANTAGONIST TOTAL PROFILE

FUNCTION OF THE TOOL

With this tool, you'll break down the details on the character who is the opponent, **trying to stop the main character** from reaching their external goal.

In general, keep in mind that the stronger your opponent is, the stronger your main character has to be to overcome them. You WANT your main character to have a big opponent, someone who is a big challenge for them in some way, because it's a bigger victory when the main character overcomes them.

Before we get into that, however, a caveat: One of the biggest mistakes novice screenwriters make is not giving the opponent any good quality.

It should not be a totally redeeming quality for the antagonist, but you want to stir up complex emotions in your audience. You do this by giving the opponent some good qualities too. This ends up making your protagonist look even better. It's also more real to life that we face enemies who are not 100% bad. Even if they are bad to us, there are other people who like them.

Adding a somewhat good quality adds dimension to the relationship between your main character and their opponent.

OPPONENT / ANTAGONIST – TOTAL PROFILE

THE TOOL

Character Name _____

What are two specific qualities of your antagonist? What are the positive and negative sides of these qualities? How do they contribute to the story?

What does your antagonist want? How does that play in his relationship with the protagonist?

How is your antagonist bonded to your protagonist? Why are they **forced** to fight in the main conflict to the end and resolve it?

What is your antagonist's greatest strength or weapon against the protagonist? How does that challenge the protagonist in the story?

What is your antagonist's underlying, real need?

How are the antagonist and the protagonist similar?

How do they differ? What is the biggest difference?

What good quality does your antagonist possess?

Describe any characteristics of specific importance. Why are these qualities significant to your protagonist? What do they reveal? Note physical appearance, social status, past relationships, psychological aspects, and so forth as appropriate. Avoid stereotypes by breaking them with a non-stereotypic characteristic. *(Reference the 3-D Characteristics Listing at the beginning of the character section.)*

Opponent / Antagonist Dialogue Profile

How would you describe the antagonist's speech pattern or rhythm? Dialect? Accent? What distinct or unusual words does this character use? Colloquialisms? Favorite phrases or words? Character tags? What distinguishes this character from the others? Feel free to reference the earlier Tool on the Protagonist's Dialogue for other ways you can make the opponent's dialogue distinct from other characters. Also reference aspects of what you just wrote in their Total Profile.

In the character's voice, write SAMPLE DIALOGUE discussing how he fits in the story.

Read the dialogue aloud. Does it sound authentic, as a person would speak? How could you make it more interesting, revealing, and concise?

LOVE INTEREST & ALLY - TOTAL PROFILES

FUNCTION OF THE TOOL

In this tool, you get an opportunity to break down two key characters who support your main character. Typically, they are embroiled in the main plot *(ally)* or a secondary storyline *(love story)*. Not always and not always for both, but you definitely need a confidant and supporter for the main character. We'll proceed as if you have both, but please adapt the function as it fits in your particular story.

Typically, there is a subplot with a Love Interest , but it could also be with a family member or friend with whom some issue from the past hasn't been worked out.

On the following pages, you'll find two profiles – one for a love interest and one for an ally. If you don't currently have both, then definitely think about adding them as they serve important purposes in the story.

The ***love interest*** is important because as human beings, most people *(audiences)* want love. But romantic relationships are also a primary source of conflict in life, so it's good for drama! You can set up a lot of conflict by having a love interest subplot in your story.

The ***function of the ally or friend*** is to give us a way to learn what the main character is thinking. The ally represents the voice of reason and viewpoint of the audience. The main character can tell their ally or best friend what they're feeling and thinking about their situation or even about the date they just went on with the love interest. A friend might ask, "Why don't you just move on from that jerk?" – which the audience is thinking – and that gives the main character a chance to explain why, instead of talking to themselves like I see in a lot of scripts.

You don't have to have a strong subplot with the ally. The ally fits best in the main plot. Typically, at some point late in the second act, even the ally gives up on trying to get the protagonist to see the truth about their errant ways, their misguided ideas. When the ally gives up, the protagonist has essentially lost their best friend. All they have left is themselves. That's when we get to see what they're made of all on their own. And that is what audiences pay for... that moment.

The Love Interest and Ally have two different functions; both are very important. Fill them out as you see fit in the following profiles.

LOVE INTEREST – TOTAL PROFILE

THE TOOL

Character Name _____

What are two specific qualities of your protagonist's love interest? How do they contribute to the story?

What is your love interest's goal or desire? How does it affect her relationship with the protagonist?

What do we learn about the protagonist through her relationship with the love interest?

What about the love interest most attracts the protagonist?

In what area is the love interest vulnerable? How does this play into the relationship with the protagonist?

When does the protagonist push the love interest away, if ever?

When does the love interest finally turn against the protagonist for his actions?

How does the protagonist redeem himself with the love interest, if at all?

Describe any characteristics of specific importance for the love interest. Why are they important? What do they reveal? Note physical appearance, social status, past relationships, psychological aspects, and so forth as appropriate. Avoid stereotypes by breaking them with a non-stereotypic characteristic. *(Reference the 3-D Characteristics Listing at the beginning of this section.)*

Love Interest Dialogue Profile

Describe the love interest's speech pattern or rhythm. Do they have a dialect? Accent? What distinct or unusual words does this character use? Colloquialisms? Favorite phrases or words? Character tags? What distinguishes this character from the others? Feel free to reference the earlier Tool on the Protagonist's Dialogue for other ways you can make the love interest's dialogue distinct from other characters. Also reference aspects of what you just wrote in their Total Profile.

In the character's voice, write SAMPLE DIALOGUE discussing how she fits in the story.

Read the dialogue aloud. Does it sound authentic, as a real person would speak? How could you make it more interesting, revealing, and concise?

Notes and Ideas

ALLY / FRIEND TOTAL PROFILE

THE TOOL

Character Name _____

What are two specific qualities of your ally (your main character's closest pal)? How do these qualities contribute to the story?

What is your ally's goal or desire? How does this play in his relationship with the protagonist?

What do we learn about the protagonist through his relationship with the ally?

What qualities of your ally reflect your protagonist? What do they have in common?

What traits of your ally are in stark contrast to your protagonist? Where do they see things very differently?

Is there a point when the ally has had enough and finally turns against the protagonist for his actions? Could there be if there's not already? Describe.

Describe any characteristics of specific importance about the ally. Why are they important? What do they reveal? Note physical appearance, social status, past relationships, psychological aspects, and so forth as appropriate. Avoid stereotypes by breaking them with a non-stereotypic characteristic. *(Reference the 3-D Characteristics Listing at the beginning of this section.)*

Ally / Friend Dialogue Profile

How would you describe the ally's character's speech pattern or rhythm? Dialect? Accent? What distinct or unusual words does this character use? Colloquialisms? Favorite phrases or words? Character tags? What distinguishes this character from the others? Feel free to reference the earlier Tool on the Protagonist's Dialogue for other ways you can make the ally's dialogue distinct from other characters. Also reference aspects of what you just wrote in their Total Profile.

In the ally's voice, write SAMPLE DIALOGUE discussing how he fits in the story.

Read the dialogue aloud. Does it sound authentic, as a person would speak? How could you make it more interesting, revealing, and concise?

RELATIONSHIP MAP

Function of the Tool

The Relationship Map is designed to help you clarify, crystalize and track the evolution of your main character's relationship with up to four supporting characters. This tool often exposes relationships which have not been clearly defined as you realize you don't know how your main character feels toward one of the other characters.

By taking time to clarify them, you will get lots of ideas on how to strengthen the characters and their relationships and have them come through richer and fuller in the script.

To use the tool, there are three steps:

1. Write the Protagonist's name in the big oval on the left and up to four other characters you want to chart in the smaller ovals on the right.

2. On the arrows pointing from the main character to the each of the others, you'll write how the main character feels about them. Above the line pointing to supporting character, write the feelings or attitudes the main character has toward them at the beginning. Below the line, write the feeling the main character has toward the other character at the end of the story. This will help you assess whether the main character has evolved in the relationship.

3. Once you've identified the feelings the main character toward the others, then do the same thing from the supporting character back to the lead. Write how each one feels about the main character at the beginning and then how they feel at the end.

Once you clarify and articulate how you want the relationships to evolve, then you can strategize on how to add anything that's missing or further refine what's already there. After this tool, you'll be introduced to the Feelings Progression Snapshot tool, which will help with implementing what you see here.

If you get ambitious, you can also do a similar thing from one supporting character to another supporting character where you think it could be worthwhile.

FEELINGS PROGRESSION SNAPSHOT

Main Character toward a Supporting Character

FUNCTION OF THE TOOL

If you're in the early stages of planning your outline or story, this tool is valuable for helping you think through what key moments need to happen to develop your main character's relationships and, in turn, the character arc.

If you've already written your script and you're now analyzing how to improve it, this tool can assist you with making sure the key moments you think are on the page are indeed still there. It gives you an opportunity to locate the exact page in the script where it happens. It's especially valuable in this regard because after you do lots of editing and rewriting over time, it's very common to begin to think something is still in the script that's no longer there. I've seen this happen over and over in critiquing thousands of scripts. As some point you know your story and characters so well, that your mind fills in the gaps, even if you took the scene out two drafts ago. Using this snapshot, you'll find the exact page something happens on so you can be sure it's on the page.

The fundamental power of this tool is that it helps you develop *the <u>evolution and progression</u> of your main character in certain relationships or regarding specific storylines*. You can list up to four progressions to add plausibility to the major change that results at the end. Use what you created on the Relationship Map Tool for support.

This tool has four parts:
- Write the <u>page number </u>of the first time we see how the other character feels toward the main character.
- Write <u>what</u> that character feels.
- Write <u>why</u> (the reason, because of) he or she feels that way.
- Then describe specifically <u>how we know</u> it from the scene on that page.

EXAMPLE: On <u>page 58</u> she feels <u>angry and sad</u> because of <u>she knows he's cheating</u>. This is revealed in the scene when <u>he looks away when he says he loves her – and earlier in the script (p. 10) he made her look in his eyes when he said it</u>.

To summarize, the **Feelings Progression Snapshot** exercise helps with three aspects of development.

- By writing out several sequential moments in the story, you can make sure the story is progressing instead of having the same old dynamic playing out over and over with two characters or in a storyline.

- It helps you to confirm that what you think is on the page is still there and you didn't cut it out in the process of editing.

- It also helps make sure that the development of the character is what you want and that it is authentic – something that evolves believably instead of just changing on a dime.

Included in the following following pages are two for the Main Character toward a Supporting Character – as part of a storyline. For this, you probably should pick the two main relationships of the main character, which would be the antagonist and an ally/love interest.

The two pages after the Main Character's progression are for tracking the feelings of a Supporting Character toward the Main Character. These could be the same storylines or another one if you prefer.

FEELINGS PROGRESSION SNAPSHOT

Main Character toward Supporting Character #1

THE TOOL

Main Character: _____

Supporting Character: _____

On Page #	Character Feels	Because of	This is revealed when

Feelings Progression Snapshot

Main Character toward Supporting Character #2

THE TOOL

Main Character: _____

Supporting Character: _____

On Page #	Character Feels	Because of	This is revealed when

Feelings Progression Snapshot

Supporting Character #1 Toward The Main Character

THE TOOL

Supporting Character: _____

Main Character: _____

On Page #	Character Feels	Because of	This is revealed when

Feelings Progression Snapshot

Supporting Character #2 Toward The Main Character

THE TOOL

Supporting Character: _____

Main Character: _____

On Page #	Character Feels	Because of	This is revealed when

GENERAL DIALOGUE ANALYSIS TOOL

Function of the Tool

For each of the key characters, you did a mini-analysis of their dialogue and you were asked to write sample dialogue.

The General Dialogue Analysis tool is for a broader analysis of the dialogue. Go through the questions and make notes of anything that occurs to you off the top of your head.

Then go through the questions thinking of one character at a time. You can make notes here or go back to that character's profile and make notes in their specific dialogue profile.

Do this for as many characters as you want, but the important thing is to do it for at least your three or four key characters in the film.

General Dialogue Analysis Tool

THE TOOL

To increase your awareness, describe your own speech patterns, favorite words, exclamations, phrases, and sentence structure.

Have you imbued your characters with your own personal favorite words, phrases, and speech patterns inappropriately? Do you need to make them more distinct from your own speech patterns and from each other?

Do your characters accidentally adopt each other's style or idiosyncratic language?

Does the dialogue serve multiple purposes in each scene, such as move the story along, define character, or give needed expository information?

Where have you written expository information in the dialogue? How could you make it more interesting? Is the exposition too long? How could it be more succinct?

Notes and Ideas

Is any of your dialogue too obvious or "on-the-nose?" How could your character say it in a way that is more sub-textual as would be appropriate for them?

Is there any dialogue you can replace with <u>nonverbal</u> communication? Anything you can have the character <u>show instead of express it in words</u>?

Read each character's dialogue aloud as you imagine they would sound. Does it sound authentic, like a real person would sound? If not, rewrite it till it does.

CHARACTER AUTHENTICATION TOOL

Function of the Tool

The biggest challenge with dialogue is having the characters sound different from each other while remaining true to their specific character. In previous tools you created the foundation for their dialogue style. When you use this next one, you'll hit pay dirt in making sure their dialogue is not only distinct but also that the character comes across as real and authentic.

In this tool you will identify a real person you know *or know of* who has the same "feel" or vibe as your character.

The power of this tool is that when you imagine someone real in your head, it's far easier to write the dialogue and capture a specific vibe for your character.

When you select someone to model your character's style after, you can pick a famous person, a grade school teacher, an uncle, a pastor, a cousin, a friend... anyone you want... living or dead, famous or not, and whether you've met them or not. The critical thing is that you know how they sound in their speaking and you're clear on what is similar to them in your character.

However, do not give your character the same name! This is only a tool to help you create stronger, more distinct and real characters!

Character Authentication Tool

THE TOOL

Character Name	Quality/Qualities	Real Person Like This

Notes and Ideas

Story Structure and Plot

INTRODUCTION
TO STORY STRUCTURE AND PLOT

In this section on Story Structure and Plot, we'll use a variety of tools to break down the main story and sub-plots, and then we'll bring them together to see how they flow.

First you'll get a chance to think the plots through individually and make a note of any inflection points where "something happens" or major plot points.

Then we'll bring all of the different storylines and plotlines together to see how the energy of the whole story moves.

PLOT POINT BRAINSTORM

FUNCTION OF THE TOOL

With this tool, you'll brainstorm all of the important moments in your script that have energy around them. Include moments in the main plot and all subplots and storylines.

I call these moments *Inflection Points*; they're like a blip on the radar. These moments occur when something changes or goes a different way than expected.

Moment like these can include when news is announced by a character. There may be a big conflict about an issue or something might come to a head. Typically, some kind of conflict will be involved, whether big or small.

This tool is for brainstorming and capturing all of those moments. Just write a simple reference to the moment something happens. Don't worry about putting the points in order, we just want them to be listed--anything you think of that where there is an emotional charge or change.

Once you've done that, you'll go to the Plot and Subplot Individual Structure Graph where you'll start to map it out and do some more planning with it.

Plot Point Brainstorm

THE TOOL

MAIN PLOT STORYLINE		
Storyline 1		
Storyline 2		
Storyline 3		

STRUCTURE OF INDIVIDUAL STORYLINES

FUNCTION OF THE TOOL

After you've brainstormed as many emotionally-charged moments as possible, it's time to break organize them into the portion of the story they happen in.

The following chart is broken up into a three-act setup--or if you prefer, you can relate to the four quarters of the story as I described at the beginning of this book (first act (Q1), first half of second act (Q2), second half of second act (Q3), and third act (Q4).

At this point, you'll start to think about how the main plot and subplot events might impact each other as you organize them by act.

For each of the inflection points in the Plot Point Brainstorm listing, now put them in the storyline and correct quadrant of the timeline they will happen in.

SEQUENCES

FUNCTION OF THE TOOL

You've now begun to sketch out lots of activity about the main plot and the subplots or secondary storylines. Now we're going to look at the story more holistically by identifying the chronological sequences which will include all the storylines.

A sequence is a series of scenes in which a particular phase of the story happens. Thinking in sequences help your story flow better. We're going to go back to plot analysis in coming pages, but the tool on sequences is placed now because we want to think through the overall flow of the story before nailing down specific moments of the plot and subplot storylines.

Each sequence should have a beginning, middle, and end. It should have two main parties involved and have a conflict between them. The sequence should end with things in a different state than when it began. In other words, there should be some kind of twist – big or small -- to move things forward. Conflict should always produce some kind of twist and movement of the plot.

Thinking in sequences will help your story to flow. In this tool, think of the major sections/sequences of your story, then write a reference name for that sequence on the tool. It might be something like: "Josh goes to the fair, makes his wish to be big, and wakes up in an adult man's body." Or simply: "Josh makes his wish at the fair and wakes up big."

To identify your sequences, practice telling your story aloud with just a summary reference to each section.

By telling the story according to sequences, you'll start to make sure it flows and is not choppy. Another key is to keep trying to capture your story in sequences until you can tell it only by referencing the main action of the sequence.

Generally speaking, you'll have seven or eight major sequences and they'll be about 10 to 12 or 15 pages long. Think of the biggest, most charged moments in your story as possible endings/beginnings of your sequences.

Sequences

THE TOOL

Tell your story as a series of sequences. Write a simple title to refer to each of them by here. Describe them fully on a separate document if you like.

- _____
- _____
- _____
- _____
- _____
- _____
- _____
- _____
- _____
- _____
- _____

STORY STRUCTURE NARRATIVE BREAKDOWN

FUNCTION OF THE TOOLS

This next three tools work closely together to build on our previous work of identifying inflection points and the act they happen in as well as our list of sequences.

First we're going to analyze Story Structure and have you narratively explain all of the key structural moments in the main story.

In the previous tools, you were only referencing points in the structure. In the Story Structure Narrative Breakdown, you'll get a chance to explain certain points narratively, meaning like a story, to make sure it all flows and makes sense.

After that tool, you'll see the **Subplot Analysis**, which has you think through the important moments of one of the other storylines. It can be the love story if you have that or it could be another secondary story.

The third tool in this part, the **Subplot Support To Main Plot Analysis**, will help you analyze the effectiveness of how the Subplot Storyline complements the Main Plotline.

Story Structure Narrative Breakdown

THE TOOL

What is the **central question**? What is the question that the story attempts to answer at every major plot point throughout the script?

Inciting Incident - What event kicks the story into action within the first ten pages?

Act I – Setup: What questions and situations are set up in the first act? (Usually takes up about the first 1/4 of the script, 25-30 pages.)

First Plot Point: What is the first major turning point or reversal that kicks the story in a different direction? Around 25% through the story and the central question is raised again.

Act II – Conflict: What conflicts arise between the protagonist and antagonist that lead to a seemingly insolvable problem? this happens in the "middle-half" of the script.

Notes and Ideas

Midpoint: What kind of plot twist or surprise happens about 50% of the way through the story, the middle point of the second act?

Second Major Twist or Plot Point: What is the second major turning point or reversal that spins the story in yet another direction? About 75% of the way through the story, the Central Question is raised again and the likely outcome twists back to the other direction.

Act III Resolution: The final 25% of the script.

Escalation Point: Where near the end does it appear that things are the worst yet? How could you create an escalation point if you don't have one?

Climax Point: Where does everything come to a head with the highest stakes, so that the central question is answered... and then resolved?

Main Character Arc Resolution: Where do we see the main character act with his newly learned behavior?

Subplot Analysis

THE TOOL

What two parties are involved? _____ and _____

What event kicks off the action for the subplot storyline?

What is the main problem it tries to solve?

What is the big conflict that arises between the two parties?

Where do things appear to be getting better but then get worse?

Climax Point: Where does everything come to a head with the highest stakes?

Resolution: How does the resolution of the subplot connect to the main plot?

Subplot Support To Main Plot Analysis

THE TOOL

In what way does the subplot mirror or contrast what the protagonist deals with in the main plot? How does this storyline amplify the main story or theme?

How does the climax of your subplot contribute to the climax of your main story?

Does it resolve close to the climax of the main story? How effective is it?

How does this storyline carry the theme through? How does it amplify your theme? What else does it say about your "message?"

What do we learn about the <u>protagonist</u> through this subplot?

Do you need it? Why? What does it add?

GRAPH OF STRUCTURE

<u>FUNCTION OF THE TOOL</u>

Now it's time to integrate all of the information on plot structure you've been working on. The first tool here is the Graph of Structure.

For this chart, select a different pen color for each plot and subplot or storyline. Or you could use a solid line for one and dashed line for another.

For one storyline at a time, you'll decide how much charge or energy a given plot point has and then at what page (% through the script it falls on). So if your Inciting Incident is that your main character gets fired at work and is devastated on page 3, then close to the left age (almost at the beginning), you would have your first plot point and it might have an energy of 30 to 50, depending on the impact and depending on what else happens in the story.

When you try to assess the level of energy a given point, think of the entire world of your story and ask what is the most highly-charged thing that could happen? That would be a 100. The idea is not to get wild and crazy but to just think, within reason in the world of the story, how important and highly-charged is that the given Plot Point or Moment of Change.

Put all of the points in for your main plot first, based on the "Energy Level" of the conflict or emotional charge created by that event. Then connect the points for that plot to get a rough sketch of the change of the stakes in it. After you do it for the main plot, go ahead and do it for the other storylines.

In assessing the structure, look to see whether the energy is dynamic versus staying stuck at one level. Likewise, notice any spots where your main storyline and secondary storylines parallel each other or criss-cross.

The goal is to make your whole structure interesting and dynamic.

Also note... there should be some places where a highly-charged moment on the graph belongs to both the main storyline and the sub storyline. They should share a moment that has implications for both. When you create moments like that, it is hugely impactful on the story.

STORY SETUP AND PAYOFF CHECKUP

FUNCTION OF THE TOOL

This tool offers a final checkup on the key setups and payoffs.

One of the great joys audiences experience are when something is setup at one point in the story and paid off at a later point. It's the nature of story itself. A person hears part of a story and wants to know how it ends.

I myself find that I cannot walk out of a movie not matter how bad it is. If I've invested myself in part of it, I'm going to see if it ever pays off!

This tool will ask you questions in different ways about the setups and payoffs in your script per standard structure. Additionally, you can work with foreshadowing to add extra audience satisfaction when it pays off.

Foreshadowing an event is when there is a subtle hint dropped about something that pays off later. The audience may sense it consciously or unconsciously but when it pays off later, it is very satisfying. The time between when something is foreshadowed and when it pays off keeps the audience hooked.

This tool helps you look at a few different elements of the story to keep the audience emotionally invested (hooked) into the story. To do this, the energy can't be dissipated and squandered. The story needs to be focused and moving forward. The questions in this tool will help you assess that.

Story Payoff Cross-Check

THE TOOL

What is the central question? In the first 10 pages, where exactly do you reveal what the central question is, the overriding goal of the main character, the context of the story?

Can you intensify your story by narrowing the time frame the story happens in?

What events or character actions do you foreshadow? Where do they pay off? Are all setups paid off? Where could you add a small foreshadow to keep the audience hooked until they find out what it means?

How can you make the beginning and ending mirror each other in some way?

What problem(s) does your ending resolve? Are all problems, issues, and subplots resolved?

How could you make your climax even more significant and impactful?

How could you milk the ending for all the emotion that remains to be felt? Is there anything that you could add that would really amplify the final resolution? Some thematic moment that plays up the emotion between the two main characters at the end?

Do you spend more than three pages on the resolution after the climax? If yes, how could get it done in no more than three pages?

Raising the Mountain

BEYOND CLICHÉ - BRINGING A SCENE TO LIFE

FUNCTION OF THE TOOL

Screenwriters sometimes – too often – put scenes in their script to either fill the pages or ones that simply don't add to the whole story. This puts a drag on the story since it's standing still and can even cause confusion for the reader as they wonder what they're missing. For any scene you feel is stagnant, use the following tool to breathe new life into it.

Beyond Cliché - Bringing A Scene To Life

THE TOOL

What is the purpose of this scene in the overall story? How are you trying to accomplish this purpose? Is the purpose of the scene accomplished?

What's the vibe of the scene at the beginning and what is it at the end? What is the arc? What conflict is in this scene and between what two parties?

What characters are involved? For each character, what is their relationship to this situation? How do they feel at the beginning of the scene? How do they feel differently at the end? How could you add some spice to make a bigger change for at least one character?

What is the main conflict? Could the stakes be raised appropriately for where this scene falls in the plotline?

Could this scene be started a few lines later or ended a few lines earlier? Can you cut a little at the beginning or at the end?

Notes and Ideas

Can you cut some of the dialogue? Can you combine a couple of things one character says?

Describe each of the following for this scene.

Plot Movement:

Character Revelation/Development:

New Information/Exposition:

Thematic Value:

EMOTIONAL FLAME-THROWER

FUNCTION OF THE TOOL

When writing a story, just as with any art, **your job is to make people feel something.**

This tool will walk you through certain points in the script to see how you can pour even more gas onto the emotion to flame up the fire.

EMOTIONAL FLAME-THROWER

THE TOOL

What is the basic emotional feeling in your story? How could you make it more intense?

Do you draw the audience in from the first page? What specifically happens in the first three pages that captivates the audience? How do you – or could you -- capture their curiosity so they **must** stay to learn the answer to some question that arises?

Where are your two biggest plot points in the story? What do you want the audience to feel then? How could you rewrite those points to take their emotions to a 10 times bigger place than you have it now? How could you amplify the emotion?

What feelings do you want the audience to experience throughout the story? When are the specific moments you want them to be feeling a certain way? Are you effective?

How could you make these moments even stronger and more emotional? How could you raise the stakes?

Where are the most emotional moments in your story? What does the main character feel? How could you make it more significant to the main character?

Does your story provide a sense of completion of the story at the end? Or do you leave questions unanswered? How does the audience feel when the story is over?

Does your ending allow the audience to feel catharsis, a sense of satisfaction? Does it lead to a new understanding about the topic, the theme? Describe the feeling at the end.

CONFLICT ESCALATAR

FUNCTION OF THE TOOL

The only way a story becomes dramatic is by the presence of conflict. It can be internal or external, but there must be a struggle between two opposing forces.

This tool will help you analyze the conflict in your story and look for spots where you can step it up.

Conflict Escalatar Tool

THE TOOL

What is the overall conflict of the story? The central question? The dramatic premise? Where does the main conflict start? What are the specific steps in which the conflict progresses, intensifies, escalates, climaxes, and resolves?

What character conflicts are present in each act? What are the <u>energy levels</u> of each of those conflicts? How could you create a greater variety of conflicts? List the major conflicts for each act.

Act 1:

Act 2:

Act 3:

What is the climax and how close to the end does it happen? How could the conflict build to a greater climax?

DOUBLING THE JEOPARDY TOOL

FUNCTION OF THE TOOL

The most important way conflict is amplified is by seeing what the characters care about and then putting that thing in jeopardy. In this tool, you'll brainstorm **what you could do** to increase the jeopardy of what the characters care about. In the next tool, you'll actually pick which things you'll use to implement it.

Audiences care about a character when they see what that character cares about, what is important to him or her.

Even in a story that's not really deep, the main character must care very much about how things go--whether it's winning a spelling bee competition, trying to get accepted into the college of their dreams, capturing the heart of the girl of their dreams, or saving the Earth from an incoming asteroid.

These are called the stakes. Your story must show what is at stake for each character involved. They need to care about what's at stake so they audiences care.

Doubling The Jeopardy Tool

THE TOOL

What is the biggest thing at stake in the main conflict? How could you raise the stakes?

What is in jeopardy for your protagonist? What is at stake if he doesn't reach his goal? What will he lose? How could it be even bigger?

Why must the protagonist reach her goal **now**? Why is it important **now** when it wasn't before? What prompted her to go for it at this time? What is the one thing that will most assuredly stop her along the way?

What other obstacles could come up for your character in this story? Play the "what if..." game and brainstorm additional obstacles. Write your three best ideas here.

Is there a "ticking bomb" in the story that creates urgency and builds tension? How could you set up the story as a race against time?

How could you increase the jeopardy by discovering that the opponent is even more powerful than first thought?

RAISING THE STAKES PLANNER

FUNCTION OF THE TOOL

In the prior two tools, you thought about and brainstormed the conflict and what was at stake.

In this tool, you now get to choose what you want to implement. Start with one idea for each act and implement that. If you want, come back and implement more ideas.

Raising The Stakes Planner

THE TOOL

For each Act's events or main conflict, how will you raise the stakes? Pick ideas from your answers on previous tools.

Act 1: _____

Act 2: _____

Act 3: _____

WRITING STYLIZER

FUNCTION OF THE TOOL

A writer who has their own unique style immediately stands out from 99% of the other writers. There's a vibe, a feel to their writing, a **way** they say things.

A screenwriter's style is different than what they say. It's the specific words they choose to describe the action. The dialogue has to be right for the characters and that's its own unique skills. But describing the action description is one of the particular places the writer's voice can shine through and set them apart.

This tool guides you in finding and expressing your voice and style in your writing. If you're witty or wry, write in that style in your scene description. If it fits for a character's dialogue, use it there, too.

The point of these questions is to have you tap into how you might begin to express your specific writing style.

Writing Stylizer

THE TOOL

What is the tone or mood of your script? What is the overall vibe you want to come through when you write the action or scene description?

How has your writing style exhibited the tone? What specific emotion or meaning-charged words have used in your description of scenes to convey the vibe?

Briefly describe your writing "style."

What type of stories do you see yourself writing long-term? Is this story representative of that?

Why are you interested in this type of story?

Go through your script and change generic verbs like **walks** to verbs that have more specific meaning like **struts** or **saunters**. Change phrases like **looks at** to **bores holes through his soul with her gaze** or **stares down**. Choose more colorful words wherever you can. Make notes here of any observations you choose.

BONUS! -- CREATIVITY TOOLBOX

THE TOOLS

The exercises listed here are to be done on a separate sheet and can be useful for breaking up feeling like you're stuck or blocked. These exercises are designed to have you look at things from a different perspective.

Write a first person account of this story from each major character's point of view.

After you write out 2 or 3 or 4 characters telling the story, see what is revealed to you about their character or possible changes you could make. If you're not unblocked yet, keep writing in first person as that character. Imagine them telling someone their backstory or having them gossip about other characters in the story. Let it roll.

Write about the relationships revealing the dimensions of the main character.

Describe how each character is connected to the main character and what we learn about the main character through him. This helps dimensionalize the main character as well as expose or clarify the purpose of the supporting characters.

Write a detailed description of your story from memory.

Highlight any questions of logic that come up. Later address and answer them.

Overall perspective. Why does each character feel they must be involved in this story?

Pick any character, even do all of them one-by-one, and write from their first person perspective as if they were explaining to a Judge why they are essential to the story. If need be, allow them to completely lie and make things up about how they have been involved in the story. Let their imaginations go wild! Plead, beg, lie, confess, reveal... anything to convince the Judge to let them stay in the story.

WRITING VISUALLY & THEMATICALLY

Notes and Ideas

SYMBOLISM - METAPHORS - VISUALS

FUNCTION OF THE TOOL

The medium of film **communicates** a story through motion pictures. While stageplays rely heavily on dialogue, being a great storyteller through film is about getting good at using pictures to tell your story.

At USC Film School – and presumably most film schools – the first short films students make are not allowed to have dialogue. The students must tell their story using only motion pictures, no character dialogue. Once they learn how to convey a story and they understand the medium of moving pictures, then they can start to add dialogue for greater nuance and complexity in the story.

The essence of filmmaking is to have the visuals tell the story and amplify the theme.
Writing scene description is not about you becoming the set decorator. Your job as the writer is to convey a vibe or the tone and other important information about the scene.

A story is enhanced, not only by the visuals of the sets and the locations, but other images that are metaphors and symbols related to the theme can be used to deepen the story and add delight for the viewer. Even if the viewer doesn't consciously notice all of the little touches, when you add them, they add depth to the overall theme.

This tool will help you dig into how you can use the set to complement and amplify the story as you describe it in your action description.

Symbolism - Metaphors - Visuals

THE TOOL

How does the location amplify the theme? Why is this location important? Could it effectively take place elsewhere? Is there a location that might add more metaphorical or archetypal meaning?

What are some recurring images, words, or phrases you could use in the action or dialogue to support the theme? What specific scenes could you add them in?

What are more visual metaphors could be associated with your theme and where could you use them? *Think of archetypal and symbolic images like birds, planes, the fall leaves, the moon, ocean waves and so on.*

What other symbols are generally related to the theme that you haven't yet used? Where might you use them?

What do you foreshadow in your story with subtle clues? What hints do you give early on about something that happens later? How could you do this at a whole new level?

Select a scene you think has good symbolic potential. What tone do you want to create through your action description? What buzz words or particular word choices set the tone of the scene? How could you add them in?

Is there a place you could add use a visual miniature that relates to the theme? *(a blueprint of a dream home, an architectural model of the grounds, a statue...)*

Are there any passageways? Tunnels? Symbolic roads? Rivers? What kind of passage do they represent in the story?

What literary devices do you use to create a tone or effect that the reader or viewer may not recognize consciously, but may be affected by subliminally? This is referring to specific words in your description. You script is meant to become a movie, but writing the description well adds delight for the reader.

How tight is your description with regard to metaphors? Does the script read fluidly without being halted by lengthy flowery writing?

MAKING LOCATIONS WORK FOR YOUR STORY

FUNCTION OF THE TOOL

Once you grasp that locations and sets are not just about the facts and logistics of where a scene takes place, you can start to choose more meaningful locations.

How many times have you seen a romantic comedy end at an airport? It's always the first image that pops into my mind when I think about a romantic comedy ending. I'm not even sure how many have actually ended there, but the point is, an airport is very symbolic of endings and new beginnings. If the partner in a romance drives off in a car, they can easily turn right back around. But once they walk away down a jetway and then we see that plane taking off... there's no turning back. It's feels much more final.

That's the power of a location.

This tool is for you to brainstorm symbolic locations and settings that fit with the theme and subject matter of your story. Once you've brainstormed some ideas, you may want to change some of the current locations to others that will be more meaningful.

Making Locations Work For Your Story

THE TOOL

Brainstorm and write down your current locations as well as other possible locations and settings that might be symbolic for your story.

EXTERIORS

_____   _____

_____   _____

_____   _____

_____   _____

_____   _____

INTERIORS

_____   _____

_____   _____

_____   _____

_____   _____

FIVE KEY LOCATIONS

FUNCTION OF THE TOOL

The purpose of this tool is to help you think through why you've chosen a given location in a visual sense.

From your list in the previous section, identify five or more key locations and write them in the next table. Then, for each of them, write what feeling you want to evoke, and then what are some images, things you could put in that location to amplify that emotion?

What visuals could you add to the scene to make the feeling even more impactful?

Key Locations

Location	General Feeling Wanted	Possible Visuals To Evoke the Feeling

LOCATION SENSATION TOOL

FUNCTION OF THE TOOL

In the last tool, we looked at how locations can naturally have certain emotions associated with them and how you could add fitting visuals to go even further.

In this tool, we want to drill down on your main location where some of the most important action happens. If you have 2 or 3 locations like that, just pick one for this exercise and do it for others on a separate sheet of paper.

This tool is to help you make sure you're clear on your main locations. If you have people coming and going from an apartment, you need to know where the door is. If something happens at a theme park, you'll need to be clear on where key structures are.

Use the outline to sketch a layout of your location to make sure that your logic of what takes place makes sense.

You'll also see a few other questions pertaining to the feel and sensations of the place.

The idea is NOT to have you be a designer but to try to make the location clear in your mind so you can create the ambience and vibe of it in your script.

Location Sensation Tool

THE TOOL

Draw a rough pencil sketch of the location you have pictured in your mind.
What is the smell, sound, texture, and temperature of this place? Describe anything that affects the five senses.

What feelings and emotions do you want to evoke here? How can you use the sensory description from above to help evoke the emotion?

What visuals would be effective, emotional, and appropriate to include here to stimulate the senses as described above?

MAKING YOUR STORY THEMATIC AND CINEMATIC

FUNCTION OF THE TOOL

In the last couple of tools, we've been looking at how locations and sets contribute to the overall impact of this visual medium.

With this tool, we're going to take another deep dive to find throughlines and images that can amplify the major themes in your story.

When you have identified possible images to associate with your story, you'll start to see places that you can put them in in fun, creative ways.

Instead of someone just looking out a window, they could suddenly see a squirrel staring back at them. Unexpected little moments like that will amplify the theme as well as surprise and delight the audience. It makes the story resonate more fully in the soul.

Making Your Story Visual and Thematic

THE TOOL

What are the major themes, topics, ideas, and issues that come up in your story?

_____ _____

_____ _____

_____ _____

_____ _____

For each of the themes and issues you listed above, identify **objects, images, metaphors, and visuals** that relate to them.

_____ _____

_____ _____

_____ _____

_____ _____

_____ _____

_____ _____

Notes and Ideas

Now for each of the themes and issues you listed above, list words, phrases, terms, that might be used in dialogue. Think of phrases also, or even coin a new one.

_____	_____
_____	_____
_____	_____
_____	_____
_____	_____
_____	_____

PRODUCTION VALUES

FUNCTION OF THE TOOL

Many screenwriters think they need to come up with the cheapest sets and locations possible because they think everyone is trying to save money on making the movie.

The truth is.... that is not always the case; it depends on what kind of movie it is.

If you're writing a low-budget horror film, sure, keep it cheap.

But if you're writing a romantic comedy, write it as is fitting to the story. Don't try to cut back.

If you're writing a big action film, then you need to add more big expensive sets and explosions. Those are called production values.

No matter what kind of budget you have, it's a good idea to try to make the movie at least LOOK more expensive by adding cool things. This tool is to get you thinking about what those things might be.

Production Values

THE TOOL

What are some unusual visuals in your script? Do you have any exceptional locations? Unusual costumes? Crawl spaces?

Are there any great spectacle scenes, such as huge parties, weddings, or celebrations?

Are there any explosions? Chases? Crashes? Stunts?

Have you created any "moments" in the production? Do you have any cinematic shots that might stick in the audience's minds forever—like Leonardo DiCaprio and Kate Winslet on the bow of the Titanic? Or maybe like the bucket of blood falling on Carrie? Where is your best bet for creating an impactful, cinematic, archetypal moment?

COMMERCIAL POSITIONING

FUNCTION OF THE TOOL

Now we're shifting gears. This tool is simply to get you thinking about marketing your script.

Even though it won't be up to you to decide who should star in your movie, thinking about it can help you think more like a producer and therefore it may lend ideas for writing roles that would appeal to stars.

Commercial Positioning

THE TOOL

Blockbusters / Successful Movies

What successful movies have been made that are similar to your script? What is special and unique about your script as compared to those already made?

Flops

Are there any big flops your story is similar to? What is different about yours that would make it successful? *(Never mention it, of course, but you need to know!)*

Name Attachments

What 2 or 3 name actors do you see being right for each major role in your script? Do you think they would want to play that type of role? Are there any particular directors or producers who might find this story appealing? Why do you think these particular people might be interested? You MUST think of A list actors, not an actor you liked who plays a secondary, recurring role on a TV show.

Notes and Ideas

MARKET APPEAL

What audience do you see this movie appealing to? What demographics? (Age, Sex, Social Status, etc.) Is the audience too small?

Think of the movies your story is similar to. Who are the individuals and production companies who made those films. Keep a running list here of movies, producers, and companies involved in those films who could potentially be interested.

Will the audience want to retell your story? Is this story easy to retell? Retell it here like you just saw it and were telling a friend about it. Make it as absolutely brief as possible. If a friend asked you, "What's it about—the basic story?" and you had to tell them in two or three lines, what would you say?

SCRIPT FORMAT & STYLING ANALYSIS

FUNCTION OF THE TOOL

For the final tool in this toolbox, we have a checklist to see if your script is ready to go to market. This is really the easiest part because it is simply yes or no whether something is correct or has been done. You have to make sure your scene headings are all caps, your dialogue needs to be roughly in the center, and so forth. And you've either done it, you haven't done it, or you need to check it. Simple.

It's the easiest part to do, yet for some reason, many screenwriters do not do it correctly!

This final checklist is a way to make sure you get the simple things out of the way so you don't lose out on a technicality, so to speak.

It is a good idea to have it proofread by a professional, but if for any reason you can't or don't, just make sure this simple part is done properly.

Script Format & Styling Analysis

THE TOOL

☐ I have removed out all camera angles, shots, and the use of "We see" at the beginning of my sentences.

☐ I have removed all cases of "begins to" and "starts to" and made the action more active by having the character actually "do it" instead of starting to or beginning to?

☐ I have you written with the active verbs ending with "s" instead of "ing"? I write "she walks and talks" instead of "she is walking and talking."

☐ My script is between 85 and 120 pages?

☐ My script is in PDF format and has a cover page with my name and contact info on it.

☐ My pages are numbered properly.

☐ Is script is typed in a courier font?

☐ Has your script been carefully proofread for grammatical and formatting errors.

☐ I am confident that of these script elements is formatted properly in my script?

____	Margins	____	Major and Minor Sluglines
____	Shots	____	Action
____	Character Cues	____	Dialogue
____	Parentheticals	____	Transitions
____	Page Numbers	____	Camera Cues
____	Sound Cues	____	Voice-Over Dialogue
____	Off-Screen Dialogue		
____	Have you minimized your use of parentheticals?		

☐ My script look easy to read and has lots of white space.

☐ I am 100% confident that my script looks professional?

Do you have any concerns about the presentation of your script?

Are there any formatting elements you need more information about? Are there specific places in the script that are non-standard that you need to figure out how it should be formatted?

TOOLBOX WRAP-UP

Congratulations. You have now completed all of the tools for analyzing your own script. You can go back to them at any time and tweak, deepen, rewrite, or add to your answers. You can also write your ideas on the tools for things you want to implement in the future for this script. Think of it as a Capture Tool for storying your ideas for development so your greatest ideas never get lost again.

Now, it's time to give yourself one big fat pat on the back for finishing this.

For a final bit of creative inspiration, read the next section for tips I gathered from a bunch of different industry professionals. These tips will continue to help you add value and pizzazz to your script.

Notes and Ideas

COLLECTED TIPS

For Better Screenwriting

- John Truby teaches a screenwriting structure that identifies 22-steps. He says, "It's important to write about something that will change your life because you may not sell it; then at least you've changed your life."

- To write a great script, you must recognize why you're writing it. Is it something you feel strongly about? Do you know what you want to say? When you know this, you can interweave your theme much more effectively, clarify the direction, and make certain decisions more consciously.

- The better you know your story and characters, the greater your clarity, and the more questions you will be able to answer. If you think through your answers as you begin, you will be more prepared to create a strong foundation for your script.

- Many of the best stories come from our own lives: experiences we've had or heard about, people we know or have known in the past, or things we've been affected by on a deep level. Look at your own life and feelings for good material.

- "Writing is rewriting" has been said many ways, many times, by many people and it's worth repeating again. Jim Boyle, Ph.D., suggests rewriting is "stress-testing your script." You must also make sure you keep a strong foundation in place as you rewrite.

- Alfred Hitchcock said, "Drama is life with the dull parts cut out." <u>Cut out all the dull parts</u> of your script.

- Structuring your story based on page number guidelines is a good tool for evaluating the pacing of your story and whether you're spending the right amount of time on particular scenes and sequences. Once you understand the pacing of the three-act structure, then you can consciously choose whether it makes sense to break the rules or not. Just don't get so caught up in the page numbers that it paralyzes you from continuing your work or makes you think your work is done because you have major plot points on page 30, 60, and 90.

- In his book <u>SCREENPLAY</u> Syd Field suggests to begin a script by working out the following major structural points in this order: Ending, Beginning, Plot Point 1, Plot Point 2. This creates the backbone that holds your story in place as you fill in the body.

- The Inciting Incident gives the story its first little push. It doesn't have to be a highly dramatic moment such as a heinous murder, it can be as simple as someone getting appointed to handle the latest case at the D.A.'s office, someone joining the Army, or a boss innocently accepting an offer to have a drink with his secretary. It's merely the kicking off point for the real story to begin.

- Drama is not about everyday ordinary life and people, it is about the exception.

- The "ghost," which indicates the main character's problem from the past, helps set up the problem in the story. It is something that has been an ongoing problem for the main character his whole life. It will affect how he deals with the issue he's about to confront in the story.

- Make your beginning and ending mirror each other. Start out with something similar to what you end with. For example, in the film "Disclosure," in the beginning Michael Douglas' character is up for a promotion. At the end, he is again eligible for a promotion. Mirroring can add artistic value and gives a sense of closure when used properly.

- Foreshadowing is suggesting or implying something early on in the script that is later manifested in full; a setup and payoff. For example, the main character receives a heart locket for her 21st birthday and we see a close-up of it as she looks it over. Then she shoves it in the drawer surreptitiously as her current lover walks in. We don't know right now why she has hidden it, but the necklace will most likely reappear later with some significance.

- Jim Boyle says "a good story creates magic and transfers energy from the page to the reader." It's the magic that makes a viewer/reader want to retell the story and watch the faces of her listeners. To check your story's energy, practice telling it succinctly and see how interested people are in hearing it from one point to the next.

- A sequence is a continuous series of scenes about the same general topic, like a chapter in a book, usually 4 to 8 pages long. For example, a "wedding sequence" might include the bride getting ready at home, the trip to the church, the ceremony, and the reception. Sequences contribute to fluidity, keep the pace moving, and help build momentum. If your script seems choppy, consider rearranging scenes into sequences.

- A sequence has a beginning, middle, and end, with a reversal, after which the plot can never go back to where it was. An event happens, something is said, a person shows up; something happens that can never be undone. This propels the story forward.

- The reversal should not fall in the same place every time in your scenes or sequences. It should sometimes be early, late sometimes, and sometimes in the middle. By varying the placement, the story is less predictable and more interesting.

- Conflict is the key, not only to an interesting drama, but also to all drama. Without conflict you have no story. Keep in mind that conflict does not have to be direct, overt hostility. It is measured on a continuum from the simplest disagreement over something such as which color tie to wear or what restaurant to go to for the evening to the most dramatic, hostile moments of angst between lovers or family members. Your script should have various types and levels of conflict to keep the story interesting.

- In a given scene each character should have a chance to "win." This will help maintain suspense and keep the audience waiting around to see how it turns out.

- Writing instructor Jeffrey Kitchen suggests that a story consists of four parts: <u>dilemma</u> (the problem), <u>crisis</u> (the character is now forced to make a decision), <u>decision and action</u> (making the decision and carrying it out), and <u>resolution</u> (the result of the decision and action).

- To build tension and momentum in your script, use a "ticking bomb," "closing doors," or "pressure cooker." Setting up the main character in a race against time creates this effect. For example, the protagonist has to get to the Mexican border before the law gets him, or parents have to find some proof of their daughter's fiancé's illegal activities before she marries the loser tomorrow.

- It is of utmost importance that the momentum in your story is not dissipated. A "ticking bomb," metaphorical or literal, helps build momentum and urgency.

- A subplot must contribute to the climax of the main story. It should not be a free-floating story that begins and ends arbitrarily. It should tie in and reflect the theme or something about the main character. Many times the subplot contrasts how another character handles the problem the main character is dealing with.

- The actual pages where the individual plot points happen in a subplot do not have generally accepted page standards comparable to those for the main plot. The subplot varies relative to a given script or story.

- Linda Seger, author of <u>MAKING A GOOD SCRIPT GREAT</u>, says that a subplot must be at least two acts long or it seems confined.

- Subplots can help strengthen and sweeten the second act in particular.

- Subplots help dimensionalize your main story, main character, and/or theme and must feed directly into the main story. Its purpose is not to arbitrarily pad your script. A good example of an effective use of subplots is "A Streetcar Named Desire." Each of the main characters has a story going on with each of the others--Blanche and Stanley, Stella and Stanley, Mitch and Blanche. "Tootsie" is also very effective with subplots.

- The love story or romance is often a subplot.

- The conflict and tension in your story should relentlessly build momentum so that at the climactic event in your story, the tension is at its highest point.

- The climax of the subplot should be near the climax of the main plot for maximum effectiveness.

- The protagonist is the character who takes action, who makes things happen. She is not passive. She has something of great importance at stake. She must drive the action and not wait for others to make decisions for her.

- The protagonist thinks that by reaching her external goal, she will be satisfied <u>internally</u> about something. However, once she reaches that goal, she learns that what she thought she wanted all along was not really important at all, now she realizes what truly is. She was really seeking to fulfill her internal need. Distinguishing between the protagonist's perceived external goal or desire and her real, internal need gives depth to the character and contributes to empathy for her.

- When a character changes from the beginning to the end of the script, as a good protagonist should, it's a slow progression, not ONE BIG CHANGE that happens all of a sudden. You should be able to identify the progressive steps of the character arc.

- Once the protagonist has come to a new realization at the end, thus completing the character arc, it is important to show him reacting with his new behavior in the old situation. This is proof for the audience that he has changed for good. This is part of the resolution in the last couple of pages.

- To give depth to your characters, make sure they have <u>choices</u>. By setting up choices which are equally valid, you create an interesting struggle for your character. The decision he makes reveals what he is all about.

- Nothing in art is trivial. Fine details in your story will help make it believable. Make sure all your facts and details about a given situation are correct. You will probably need to research something, if not many things, for your story. Just be sure to go into detail about the right things, those with thematic value.

- If you feel unmotivated, uninspired, or blocked, research your story. Research can entail going to the library for specific fact-based information on any subject that comes up in your story, or it can be as creative as researching the characters in your head by writing letters to them or from them, writing their accounts of this event. When you research, the floodgates will open up again and you can move forward in your work.

- Continuing with the topic of "details," show little things about your character which reveal big things about him. Jeff Bridges once played the role of an ex-convict in which he discovered his 12-year-old son had brought marijuana back to their hotel room. When Jeff confronted the son, the first thing he said was, "This could get me locked up again," thinking of the negative effect on himself first. Another parent may have asked, "Where did I go wrong?" A single line of dialogue can reveal a life history.

- Showing a character's "private" moment, thoughts, or feelings can help the audience identify with him. Perhaps we see a hint of guilt about something he's done that he is not yet prepared to apologize for. The other characters don't yet see this, but the audience feels closer and more empathetic now that they know he has a conscience.

- Good dialogue has <u>subtext</u>. It is not "on-the-nose." Even in real life, we do not always say what we mean. By our intonations, we may mean something altogether different than the meaning of the words alone would convey. For example, "Thanks a lot," said sarcastically. Subtext is the meaning beneath the surface of the words. Edit your dialogue to leave out what should be beneath the surface and in the subtext.

- Good dialogue <u>reveals</u> character rather than tells about it.

- Dialogue can accomplish many tasks, however, be sure that a character's growth is shown externally, not only by what is said. As in real life, actions speak louder than words.

- When you must get out lots of information or exposition in a scene, write dialogue instead of a monologue by having other characters ask questions, or mention bits and pieces of the exposition that they already know but that the audience doesn't know yet.

- The antagonist has goals that conflict with the protagonist. He will do anything to reach his own goal. The stronger your antagonist is, the stronger the protagonist must be to overcome him; therefore it's best to have an opponent that is strong in his opposition, a tough challenge.

- Because film is a visual medium, when you have a conceptual antagonist, one person should personify it. For example, identify an individual in the government as opposed to the conceptual "government." By personifying the antagonist, we can visualize the external conflict.

- Your antagonist does not have to be a hostile, head-to-head opponent. There are many ways of creating obstacles for the protagonist other than direct collisions. Some of the greatest stories ever written are about betrayal between best friends or lovers. Dona Cooper, in her book <u>WRITING GREAT SCREENPLAYS FOR FILM & TV</u>, identifies the three types of opponents as fiend (an all-out bad guy), adversary (someone who is not against the protagonist but is an obstacle), and pest (someone who is just an irritation).

- Some coaches recommend writing a first person bio, anywhere from 1-30 pages, about each character. As you write, you will get to know your character in a different way. Your character will begin to talk to you. New ideas will come from a level deep within that you hadn't consciously thought of. Try it!

- Write a letter to any character that you want to understand something more about. Elaborate on what you would like to know about them, then put the letter away, stuff it in a bottle and throw it in the river, or anything to forget about it. Shortly after you do this, your character will speak to you; you will draw answers from your subconscious that may never have occurred to you through conscious efforts.

- By making the antagonist strong and giving the audience a reason to like him in some way, or to at least get some understanding of him, the protagonist will have to be even stronger, or "better," to remain the hero. Therefore, a strong antagonist can strengthen the protagonist.

- Minimize space used on hellos, good-byes, and introductions. This type of dialogue should only be present when it leads to the movement of the plot or reveals character. Generally, it uses up valuable script space and does nothing for your story. It is one of those "real life" things that should not be done in the script.

- All dialogue must have a purpose. It should be structured to accomplish specific goals in your script. It is not written just to show people talking and what they're like. Know the purpose of each line of dialogue. Does it reveal character? Pass on needed exposition? Move the plot along? What goals does it accomplish?

- Your love interest character should reveal qualities about the main character that are unexplored elsewhere. Not all movies have a love interest subplot, but when done well, it adds depth to the main story. The love interest subplot should underscore what's happening in the main plot line.

- Some coaches theorize that physical statistics don't matter much. Although they will never all be relevant to the script, some attributes will indeed affect a character in a specific way. For example, a 6'8" man would respond differently in many situations than a 5'1" man would. Specify any detail that specifically suggests, affects, reveals, or implies something important about a character.

- Dialogue is a particular element that should not be refined until the later stages of rewriting. The big picture, the plot, should be well in place before spending time polishing the dialogue since it is the most dynamic and changeable element by its nature.

- To delineate the dialogue more effectively, picture a real person that you know of who speaks the way you see your character speaking. Then one at a time, rewrite each character's dialogue with the picture of the real person in mind. Be sure to do this for one character at a time or you will lose the benefit of doing it this way.

- It is critical to note that dialogue, even style of dialogue, comes out of character. Who your character is will dictate a specific type of dialogue. It is not an arbitrary decision.

- When there is only one main protagonist, the number one purpose of each supporting character is to reveal something about that character.

- The ally or friend of the protagonist is important because it is a way that your protagonist can reveal things about himself, what he's thinking or considering, his past, and so forth.

- The ally is someone the protagonist can talk to, someone who believes in the protagonist and his goal all along...until finally, the protagonist goes a little too far and steps over the line in trying to reach his goal. At this point the ally turns on him, gives up on him, and is finally disappointed in what the protagonist has become. When the ally, of all people, turns his back, the protagonist temporarily feels that all is lost. In his 22-step structure, John Truby calls this point "Apparent Defeat."

- Giving your ally a goal serves to quickly humanize and add dimension, which is important since you have very little time to spend on the ally in the script.

- When it comes to exposition and back-story (what happened before the script began), don't try to tell everything at once. Reveal the information throughout the script as it is needed for the plot to develop.

- Dialogue is often overwritten in arguments that are going nowhere. If an argument continues throughout a long scene, make sure it escalates. Many times, the dialogue goes back and forth with no progress (like in real life), assuring the death of the scene.

- When the dialogue feels too lengthy or drawn out, it is probably failing to move the story along, reveal character, or give needed expository information. Change some of it to action. Minimize how much of the story happens through dialogue instead of action.

- The dialogue must sound real, but it is not real. It must be <u>distilled</u> for the screenplay form. It must relate to the story, the theme. If it is expository, try to have it accomplish other goals as well, such as lead to more conflict.

- Dialogue can do several things at once: move the plot along, deliver exposition, reveal character, support or connect with the visuals, or indicate the subtext beneath the surface.

- Have a "reading" of your script to test the authenticity of the dialogue. It's best to do the reading with professional actors who will give input, but even a reading with friends can be beneficial. Assign which characters each person will read the dialogue for and assign another person to do the narration, which includes reading the scene headings and action.

- Why does Hollywood like "up" or happy endings? Natural human psychology craves and appreciates catharsis. Good movies allow us to work vicariously through a problem to its resolution, which feels good since so many things in our daily lives are not resolved.

- Unclear endings can be unsettling. Before choosing a tragic, sad, or unclear ending, consciously think through the specific emotional effect of your choice and decide if that's what you really want to say and want the audience to feel.

- Emotions in a script happen on two levels--one is that which the character feels in the story, and the other is that which the audience feels. When the audience feels the same emotion as the character, it is a PRIMARY emotion. When the audience feels something different than the character, it is a SECONDARY emotion. To create an empathetic character, work toward affecting primary emotions.

- A good writer uses any trick in the book, or <u>not</u> in the book, to get the audience to feel a certain way. The challenge is to not let the tricks show, to hide the seams of the writing.

- Does the story work on the emotions of the audience throughout? That's the key to writing a great screenplay. The challenge in writing is making that happen.

- The visuals you describe in detail in your script should evoke specific emotions, not be haphazardly chosen. The description should be short and pointed when describing the general setting, while allowing more time for describing that which has particular meaning in the script.

- Effective use of symbolism adds texture to your screenplay. Symbols can be anything in the background: furnishings, paintings, ambient sounds; they can be repeated words, phrases, visuals, religious items, or anything that effects a subliminal resonance. It is important to keep in mind that any symbols which are part of the environment, and specifically related to the character, must be consistent with his background. (For example, you wouldn't have a cross, a Holy Bible, and a painting of Jesus Christ around the fireplace in a Buddhist's home.)

- Adding symbolism can be lots of fun, but the writer must be cautious to not step over the fine line and direct the movie. Symbolism must be subtly woven in, taking care to avoid having too many boring details about what is in the background.

- When a script is formatted incorrectly, has the wrong number of pages, or contains grammatical errors, it makes a bad first impression. When the reader sees the script is not professionally finished, he may assume the story itself is less than professional. It's like a car with a custom-built engine and a rusty primer-coated body. It looks crappy on the outside, but it's got power to move you; however some people won't look beyond the outside.

- After investing a tremendous amount of time in writing your script, it is critical to spend a little more to make sure it is formatted properly. The Smart Girls publication <u>FORMATTING YOUR SCRIPT HOLLYWOOD STYLE (And The Reasons Behind The Rules)</u> gives specific details on formatting every element in a script, along with tips on developing your writing style.

- In THE AMERICAN HERITAGE COLLEGE DICTIONARY "deus ex machina" means "an unexpected, artificial, or improbable character, device, or event introduced in a work of fiction or drama to resolve a situation." Make sure that your ending is not an act of God or Fate because it strips the protagonist of his power.

- "All drama really boils down to something very simple: Resolving a conflict between this one and that one," by Melody Jackson.

GLOSSARY

Ally - usually is best friend; someone who the main character can talk to

Antagonist - opponent; the main character creating obstacles for the protagonist

Catharsis - the relief of tension and anxiety by bringing repressed feelings and fears to consciousness

Central Question - the question the story raises at the beginning and answers at the end

Climax - the highest point of conflict or tension in the story; the point the story has been building to from the beginning

Conflict - the clashing of two parties; not always a direct, head-on collision; divergent goals

Desire - what the protagonist thinks he wants; his external goal

Escalation Point - a false climax when it appears things will be resolved but the stakes are raised instead

Exposition/Expository Information - in reference to dialogue it is answering who, what, when, where, why, and how about something or someone not in the scene.

Goal - what the protagonist is striving to achieve externally; desire

Hook - catchy, unique situation or circumstance that makes the story interesting and/or makes people want to watch; something about the story that catches the audience's attention

Mirroring - similar events or scenes that happen at the beginning and the end of the story

Need/Dramatic Need - the protagonist's internal goal; what he realizes at the end of the story

Premise - the foundation of the story; the writer's belief about what the story proves

Protagonist - the main character whose story is being told; lead; hero; character of focus

Reversal - Aristotle's term for a major change in the direction of the story

Rhyming - repeating images, words, symbols in the story

Resolution - the answer to the central question

Sequence - a series of scenes revolving around one main topic

Shift-Point - the term for the point in a sequence, after which the story can never go backward; Aristotle calls it the "reversal"

Stakes - what stands to be lost or gained, usually in reference to the protagonist

Subtext - the underlying message in a character's dialogue; what is not said, but is meant

Symbolism - visuals, metaphors, or themes in your story; especially those which are recurring

Theme - the topics or issues the story brings up

Tone - the feeling created by the story as you read it--upbeat, sad, dark, ominous, cavalier...

Unity of Opposites - the unbreakable bond between two opposites; a situation or circumstance which brings them together and demands a resolution

Dear Screenwriter,

Before you finish, I want to thank you!

Thank you for purchasing and reading this book. I am here to help you with the information I compiled in this book, and I also take it as a compliment that you have chosen to read what I put together.

I have always been passionate about helping screenwriters because you have to tap deep into your soul to look at a blank page and start typing a story that you have somewhere within.

Whether it's the courage it takes to pour your heart out on the page, the diligence it takes to flesh out a whole story and work on it, the guts it takes to send your script to an analyst for review or to a contest for consideration, or the creativity it takes to create the character of a lifetime, I honor your work and what it takes to write a screenplay. It is my pleasure to be of service to you.... it always has been. Thank you again for letting me be a part of your creative journey.

Melody Jackson, Ph.D.

ADDITIONAL RESOURCES BY MELODY JACKSON

SCRIPT ANALYSIS BY MELODY JACKSON

http://smartg.com/script-coverage/

At some point in the process of rewriting your script -- even after using this guide -- you will get to the point where you want someone else to give you an outside view of how your script development is coming along as a whole work. We definitely recommend that when you get to that point you enlist the professional services of a top script analyst like Dr. Melody Jackson *(the author)* to be that outside reviewer.

Melody is a compassionate, insightful, and articulate script analyst and coach who fully engages with writers as she guides them to fulfill the potential of their screenplays. She asks questions and listens and tunes in to both the said and the unsaid for that guidance. Melody believes that every writer writes to tell a story that matters. She guides them to deliver that story in the most impactful and marketable way possible.

In her script analysis process Melody reviews it from two critical fronts. One front is a structural analysis that draws from the classical tradition of Aristotle, the essence of the hero's journey as revealed by Joseph Campbell, and a variety of contemporary theories on story structure. The second front, which may be the more important of the two, is listening for **what moves the audience emotionally** in the story. Melody's doctorate is in Mythological Studies and in her dissertation *The Mythic Power of Film*; she discovered four dimensions through which the medium of film impacts audiences so profoundly.

On three different occasions over an 11-year period, *Creative Screenwriting* magazine rated Melody one of the **top 5 script analysts** in the country. Melody has critiqued literally thousands of stories in depth, many of which have gone on to win awards and lead to deals for the writer.

Melody's overall screenwriting philosophy is reflected in this workbook. For more information on working with Melody directly on developing your screenplay *(reasonable rates)*, go to our website:

Go to our website at: smartg.com
Or email us at support@smartg.com
Or call us directly at (818) 907-6511

INSPIRATIONS & RECOMMENDATIONS

Blacker, Irwin R. *Elements of Screenwriting, The*. Macmillan Publishing Co., 1986.

Cooper, Dona. *Writing Great Screenplays For Film and TV*. Prentice-Hall, 1994.

Egri, Lajos. *Art of Dramatic Writing, The*. Simon & Schuster, 1960.

Field, Syd. *Screenplay*. Dell Publishing, 1982.

Goldman, William. *Adventures in the Screen Trade*. Warner Books, Inc., 1983.

Jackson, Melody. *Formatting Your Script Hollywood Style* (And the Reasons Behind the Rules). Smart Girls Publishing. 1995.

King, Viki. *How To Write A Movie In 21 Days*. Harper and Row Publishing, 1988.

Kosberg, Robert. *How To Sell Your Idea To Hollywood*. Harper Perennial, 1991.

McKee, Robert. *Story*. HarperCollins Publishers, 2010

Seger, Linda. *Creating Unforgettable Characters*. Henry Holt and Company, Inc., 1990.

Seger, Linda. *Making A Good Script Great*. Samuel French Trade, 1987.

Snyder, Blake. *Save the Cat*. Michael Wiese Productions, 2005.

Truby, John. *The Anatomy of Story: 22 Steps to Becoming a Master Storyteller*. Farrar, Straus and Giroux, 2008.

Vogler, Christopher. *The Writer's Journey: Mythic Structure for Storytellers & Screenwriters*. Michael Wiese Productions, 1992.

Whitcomb, Cynthia. *Selling Your Screenplay*. Crown Publishers, 1988.

Wolff, Jurgen, and Kerry Cox. *Top Secrets Of Screenwriting*. Lone Eagle Publishing, 1993.

Additional Resources for Screenwriters

Screenplay Marketing Services, Typing, Proofreading and Script Analysis Services can be found on our website for Smart Girls Productions at:

smartg.com

Educational Resources on Marketing Your Script and the Craft of Screenwriting can be found on or Hollywood Business School website at:

hollywoodbschool.com

FREE GIFT!

As a final gift to you, please get your FREE PDF copy of

21 Ways To Make Your Script More Commercial

on our website at

smartg.com/21-ways-an

Made in the USA
Middletown, DE
23 December 2019